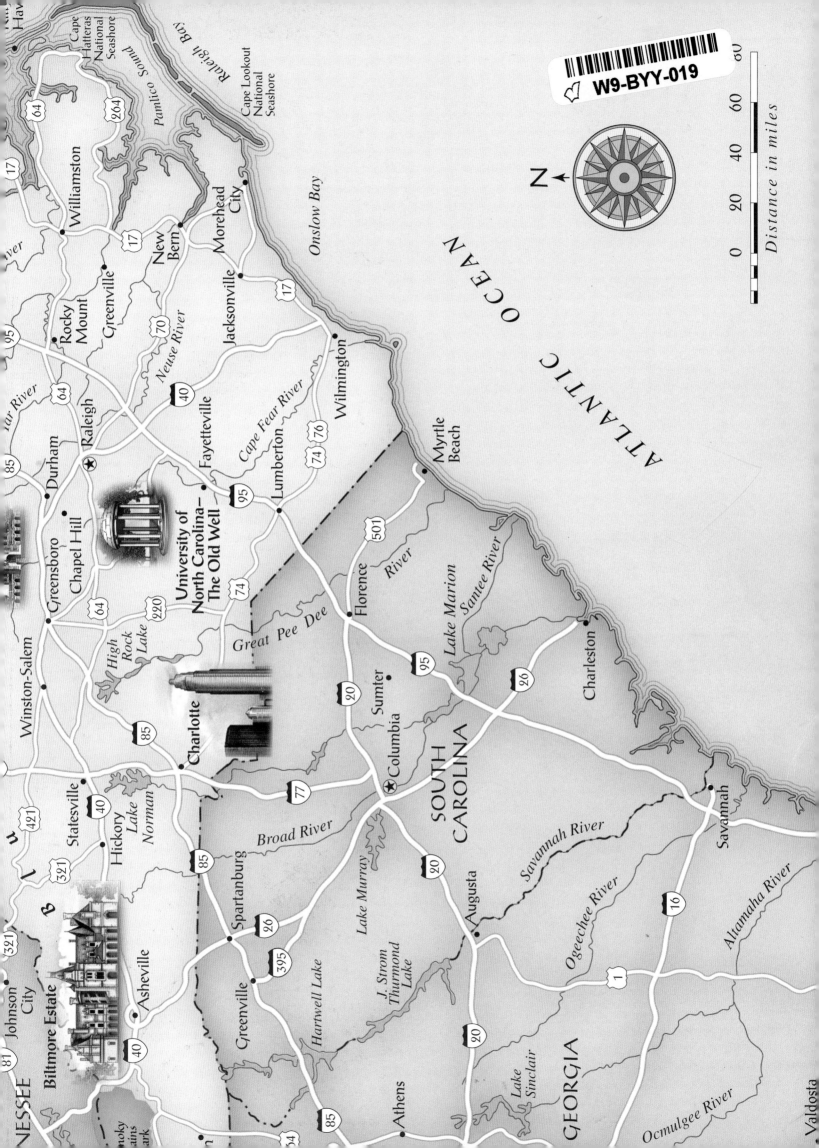

ATLANTIC OCEAN

Distance in miles

N

60

60

40

20

0

TENNESSEE

Johnson City

81

321

Biltmore Estate

Asheville

40

Smoky Mountains Park

421

Statesville

321

Hickory

Lake Norman

40

Spartanburg

85

Greenville

26

395

Hartwell Lake

Athens

85

54

Lake Sinclair

GEORGIA

Ocmulgee River

1

20

Augusta

Savannah River

J. Strom Thurmond Lake

Lake Murray

20

Ogeechee River

16

Altamaha River

Savannah

Winston-Salem

Greensboro

Chapel Hill

Durham

Raleigh

85

64

220

High Rock Lake

Charlotte

85

77

Broad River

Columbia

SOUTH CAROLINA

Sumter

20

95

26

Charleston

Lake Marion

Santee River

Florence

River

501

Great Pee Dee

74

University of North Carolina— The Old Well

Fayetteville

95

Lumberton

74 76

Cape Fear River

40

Neuse River

70

Rocky Mount

Greenville

Williamston

95

64

64

17

Haw

Cape Hatteras National Seashore

264

Pamlico Sound

Raleigh Bay

Cape Lookout National Seashore

New Bern

17

Morehead City

Jacksonville

17

Onslow Bay

Wilmington

Myrtle Beach

CAROL M. HIGHSMITH AND TED LANDPHAIR

NORTH CAROLINA

A PHOTOGRAPHIC TOUR

CRESCENT BOOKS

NEW YORK

This 1998 edition is published by Crescent Books®, an imprint of Random House Value Publishing, Inc., 201 East 50th Street, New York, N.Y. 10022.

Crescent Books® and colophon are registered trademarks of Random House Value Publishing, Inc.

Random House
New York • Toronto • London • Sydney • Auckland
http://www.randomhouse.com/

Printed and bound in China

Library of Congress Cataloging-in-Publication Data
Highsmith, Carol M., 1946–
North Carolina /
Carol M. Highsmith and Ted Landphair.
p. cm. — (A photographic tour)
Includes index.
ISBN 0-517-18605-5 (hc: alk. paper)
1. North Carolina—Tours. 2. North Carolina—Pictorial works. 3. North Carolina—Description and travel. I. Landphair, Ted, 1942– .
II. Title. III. Series: Highsmith, Carol M., 1946– Photographic tour.
F252.3.H54 1998 97–37125
917.5604´43—dc21 CIP

8 7 6 5 4 3 2

Project Editor: Donna Lee Lurker
Designed by Robert L. Wiser, Archetype Press, Inc., Washington, D.C.

All photographs by Carol M. Highsmith unless otherwise credited: map by XNR Productions, page 5; The Ruth McKinney Collection, page 6; The James Walsh Collection, page 8; Durham Convention & Visitors Bureau, page 9; North Carolina State Archives, page 10; Wilson Library, University of North Carolina at Chapel Hill, page 11; The Ruth McKinney Collection, page 12 and 13; The Krispy Kreme Corporation, page 14; Old Salem, Inc., page 15; Mast General Store, Valle Crucis, page 16; The Ed Bond Collection, page 17; Pack Memorial Library, Asheville, page 18; The Biltmore Estate, page 19; Tufts Archives of the Given Memorial Library, page 20; Special Collections and Archives, Wright State University, page 21

THE AUTHORS GRATEFULLY ACKNOWLEDGE THE SUPPORT PROVIDED BY

HILTON HOTELS CORPORATION

AND

THE CHARLOTTE HILTON AT UNIVERSITY PLACE
THE NORTH RALEIGH HILTON
THE WILMINGTON HILTON

IN CONNECTION WITH THE COMPLETION OF THIS BOOK

THE AUTHORS ALSO WISH TO THANK THE FOLLOWING FOR THEIR GENEROUS ASSISTANCE AND HOSPITALITY DURING THEIR VISITS TO NORTH CAROLINA:

Sara Akerlund

J. P. and Nancy Carter

Nancy Fowler

Ruth McKinney

Vivian Overby

Mary Ruth Pryor

Asheville Convention & Visitors Bureau

Boone Convention & Visitors Bureau

Burlington/Alamance County Convention & Visitors Bureau

Cape Fear Coast Convention & Visitors Bureau

Chapel Hill/Orange County Visitors Bureau

Charlotte Convention & Visitors Bureau

Craven County Convention & Visitors Bureau

Durham Convention & Visitors Bureau

Historic Edenton

Greensboro Area Convention & Visitors Bureau

High Point Convention & Visitors Bureau

North Carolina Division of Travel and Tourism

Outer Banks and Dare County Tourist Bureau

Greater Raleigh Convention & Visitors Bureau

Rockingham County Tourism Development Authority

Winston-Salem Convention & Visitors Bureau

Comfort Suites Waterfront, New Bern

First Colony Inn, Nags Head

NO ONE EVER THOUGHT TO CALL NORTH CAROLINA "Long Carolina," but the name would have fit. It's five hundred miles from its barrier islands, which elbow far out into the Atlantic Ocean, to the western tip of the state, high in the rugged Great Smoky Mountains, farther west than Detroit. Until Tennessee was carved out in 1789, North Carolina, which is shaped a bit like the pilot's wings presented to children on airplane flights, was once even longer, stretching all the way to the Mississippi River. Once one of the South's most backward regions, "Carolina," as its residents love to call it—as if the "other" Carolina to the south were a yokel cousin—is now the mid-South's most industrial and technologically progressive state.

It is also one of the nation's most temperate, scenic, and historic places—America in miniature in many ways. In this single state, one can visit a shoreline so fearsome that it is called the "Graveyard of the Atlantic," mountain forests so dense that not even a county road can be found for miles around, and a swamp whose very name, Dismal, says everything about its bleakness. North Carolina is also home to exquisite colonial mansions and Civil War battlefields, tobacco and cotton fields, ribbons of superhighways decorated with bedazzling median wildflowers, energetic middle-sized cities, and manicured research parks that are the envy of other states.

North Carolina has grown so fast that it has passed even Virginia and Georgia in population. Almost twice as many people live in North as in South Carolina, in part explaining the smugness North Carolinians exhibit toward their neighbors. While Virginia and South Carolina have clung to their romance with old, genteel ways, North Carolina exemplifies the robust New South.

Yet, at one time, it seemed the most unlikely southern state to prosper. North Carolina had less moneyed wealth than other states of the Old South. Poor but fiercely independent Scots-Irish, Germans, and English Quakers staked out small, red-dirt farms in the piedmont plateau, and later the mountain valleys, promoting planter-east versus farmer-west sectionalism. Many of them had arrived seeking religious freedom or the right to be left alone. Dubious about provisions in the new federal Constitution calling for a strong central government, North Carolina was the second-to-last original colony to ratify the document—almost two years after Delaware had been the first to do so. In 1785 there was even an attempt to create a new state, called "Franklin," in the North Carolina uplands. The insurgents wrote a constitution that forbade doctors, preachers, and lawyers from being members of the legislature and named John Sevier governor. Sevier was hunted down and arrested by state authorities, who charged him with treason. The Franklin idea collapsed when neither the Continental Congress nor any other states recognized the rump state. During his trial in Jonesboro, Sevier escaped, and no one bothered to pursue him. The "Franklin" counties were later included in territory lopped off to form Tennessee, and Sevier was elected its first governor.

North Carolina was first visited by Europeans in 1524, when Giovanni da Verrazzano, a Florentine leading an expedition financed by King Francis I of France, paused along the Outer Banks on his way north, where he would gain far more fame exploring what would one day be called New York Harbor. Two years later, Spaniards sailed from Santo Domingo to the mouth of the "Rio Jordan"—probably the Cape Fear River—claimed the territory for Spain, and left. Spanish maps thereafter included the Carolinas in Spanish Florida, though Spanish colonists never ventured much farther north than Saint Augustine. In 1540 the peripatetic Spanish explorer Hernando de Soto, who tramped through the mid-South on his way to discovering the Mississippi River, got as far east as the Carolina mountains.

Raleigh artist Elizabeth Edwards was largely self-taught. Among her subjects was this painting of nineteenth-century rustic cabins in rural Rockingham County—to which North Carolina's extended Carter family still repairs each June for a massive family reunion. A recent such gathering is pictured on page 79.

So the mid-Atlantic region was left to the British to colonize. Walter Raleigh, a wealthy London businessman armed with a commission from Queen Elizabeth I, financed an expedition to find suitable settlement sites. Raleigh never journeyed to the New World, but on their first mission his commanders got as far as Roanoke Island in the sound to the west of the Outer Banks. They poked around the region, found the Indians to be hospitable, and sailed for home, bringing with them two "lustie men, the Indians Manteo and Wanchese" and glowing descriptions of "sweete, fruitfull and wholesome" land. So pleased was Queen Elizabeth with their report that she knighted Raleigh, who promptly christened the new territory "Virginia" in honor of the Virgin Queen. Soon afterward the first colonists—108 men—arrived in Virginia. They planted the Union Jack on Roanoke Island and built Fort Raleigh. But they spent too much time searching for gold and not enough time farming. After a year of meager rations and skirmishes with the Native Americans—who proved to be not so friendly after all—the colonists abandoned Roanoke Island and sailed for home on the ships of Sir Francis Drake, bringing with them the first tobacco, white potatoes, and Indian corn to be seen in England. Another British ship came upon the deserted fort, so its commander left behind fifteen men to preserve the English claim. In 1587 a second colony of ninety-one men, seventeen women, and nine children, sent by Raleigh, arrived on Roanoke Island. There the governor's daughter, Eleanor Dare, gave birth to a daughter, Virginia, the first English child born in the New World. The governor, John White, headed back to England to procure supplies, but his return to Virginia was delayed by menacings from the Spanish Armada. When he finally arrived in 1590, the colonists had disappeared without a trace, save for the word "CROATOAN" carved on one tree and the letters "CRO" on another. The fate of this "Lost Colony" has been conjectured ever since. What happened to the settlers? Hostile Indians? Starvation? A hurricane? An ill-fated trip inland?

In the decades that followed, marshy, tidewater lowlands far north of Roanoke Island became Virginia's first permanent settlement of Jamestown, and colonization proceeded west rather than southward. What is now North Carolina was not revisited by Englishmen until 1622.

Duke University founder James Buchanan Duke wanted this towering, Gothic-style chapel to "have a profound influence on the spiritual life of the young men and women who come here."

Seven years later, King Charles I granted "Carolana"—the Land of Charles, extending (on paper) as far west as "the South Seas"—to his attorney general, Sir Robert Heath. But with stories about the Lost Colony still abounding, Heath failed to recruit any colonists. Eventually northern Carolana was sparsely settled by farmers drifting down various streams from Virginia, while a second, far more successful, settlement took root around Charleston harbor. In 1691 a governor took up residence in thriving, sophisticated Charleston. A deputy was dispatched to keep an eye on northern Carolina, which languished. Virginia ports refused to ship its tobacco, Indians preyed upon settlements, and pirates, including Edward Teach—Blackbeard—plundered ships off the coast almost at will. Upper Carolina did not even get its first town—tiny Bath—until 1705 or independent colonial status as "North Carolina" until 1712. In 1729 King George II purchased most of the shares of its indolent proprietors, and he turned the territory into a royal colony. New Bern, on the Neuse River midway between Albemarle Sound and the South Carolina line, became the colonial capital, and "New Liverpool"—later called Wilmington—evolved into the principal port. North Carolina society fell into four strata: wealthy

On the billboard:

ROLL YOUR OWN
AND SAVE YOUR ROLL
GENUINE 5¢
'BULL' DURHAM
TOBACCO

THE ORIGINAL–ESTABLISHED 1867
THE MAKINGS OF A NATION~

planters, living on a few large plantations along lowland rivers and Albemarle Sound; hardy pied-mont farmers; indentured servants, including convicts sent from England to work off their sentences; and black slaves, who often outnumbered whites in the eastern counties. There were no public schools, but the wealthy were taught by tutors and sent to college in Virginia, New England, and Great Britain; and a widespread apprenticeship system taught trades to the lower classes.

Like other British New World colonies, North Carolina eventually revolted against the King's rule, and on April 12, 1776—having already sent the royal governor packing—a provincial congress became the first among the colonies to declare "Independency." North Carolina patriots fought the British and their Cherokee Indian allies during the American Revolution and eventually forced Lord Earl Charles Cornwallis into a retreat to Wilmington. From there, Cornwallis marched north into Virginia and his ultimate defeat at Yorktown.

State officials ceded the ungovernable far-western counties to the Union as the new state of Tennessee and settled into a period of agrarian sustenance. Having met in seven other cities during the Revolutionary War, the General Assembly bought one thousand acres near Wake Court House and laid out a new city, Raleigh, as the permanent seat of state government. The new brick capitol burned in 1831 and was replaced by the present building in 1840.

Stripped of tens of thousands of its residents who tried their luck in the nation's great westward expansion, mired in several agricultural recessions, invaded in the Civil War and deprived of forty thousand of its young men killed in that conflict, North Carolina was long looked upon as an economic backwater—the "Rip Van Winkle of the States." In 1815 it had no large port, one cotton mill, only twenty-three small iron works, and a few small gristmills and distilleries. And as late as 1860, it had only two cities with a population over 5,000—Wilmington and New

In North Carolina tobacco country near Durham, the makers of the Bull Durham brand came up with a novel mode of advertising their chewing and "roll your own" cigarette tobacco by sending forth a rolling promotion, pulled by an obliging steer.

Unlike mountainous western North Carolina, the eastern lowlands get few troublesome snowfalls. But Raleigh got a corker of a storm in 1899. Shopkeepers labored to clear Fayetteville Street.

Bern. Even North Carolina's nickname—the Tar Heel State—grew out of its backwoods image, for shoeless hill folk boiling sap into pitch and turpentine in the piney woods invariably tracked home tar on their heels. (A more colorful explanation ties the nickname to the Civil War, when North Carolina regiments were said to hold their ground in fierce fighting as if their heels were stuck in place by tar.)

Facing the real prospect of a revolt in its western counties, the General Assembly finally agreed to modify the state constitution in 1835, allowing for the popular election of the governor, fair reapportionment of legislative seats, and the beginnings of public-school education for all of its white citizens. To make up for the lack of public colleges, religious sects established their own: Trinity College—later Duke University—(Methodist), Wake Forest College (Baptist), Davidson College (Presbyterian), and Salem Female Academy (Moravian) among them.

At first North Carolina, which had a number of active abolitionist societies and generally defended slavery only as a necessary economic evil, was lukewarm to calls for secession. Only after the Union mustered troops following the firing on Fort Sumter on May 20, 1861, and engaged Confederate troops at Bull Run, did North Carolina join the Confederacy. Thus it was the second-to-last state to leave the Union, much as it had been the second-to-last original colony to join it. Other southern states bore the brunt of battle in the Civil War, though eleven major battles were fought on North Carolina soil.

The collapse of the Confederacy cost North Carolina dearly, not only in lives and property lost and in the breakup of plantations into meager tenant farms, but also in the difficult adjustment to the emancipation of 350,000 slaves who had been the working backbone of its economy. But the twentieth century brought a remarkable transformation. Better schools and

roads, new power plants, furniture mills, and other factories sprang up across the state. So did the textile and paper industries, whose cheap nonunion workforce, ample supplies of water, and generous tax breaks lured towel, hosiery, denim, and paper mills from the North, devastating the economy of Massachusetts in particular. With the discovery of "bright tobacco"—a sweet leaf that could be raised in porous, sandy soil, tobacco became North Carolina's largest cash crop, and cigarette-manufacturing plants grew up in Durham, Winston, Wilson, and Reidsville. At Rocky Mount, a radio station signed on with call letters apropos of the town's tobacco economy: WEED. Soon the yeoman class of farmers and factory workers came to dominate North Carolina, bringing an air of pragmatism and unpredictability to politics and policies. In later years the state would elect both unmitigated liberal governors like Terry Sanford and unbending conservative U.S. senators like Jesse Helms.

The University of North Carolina at Chapel Hill became an intellectual powerhouse. In *Inside U.S.A.,* John Gunther called it "the single most noteworthy thing in the state." Duke University in Durham, called Trinity College before the influx of millions of dollars in tobacco money, also attracted scholars and top students from around the country. Military training facilities during both world wars, a growth in tourism, the development of Charlotte as a regional banking center, and the creation of a Research Triangle through the combined efforts of Duke, UNC–Chapel Hill, and North Carolina State University invigorated the state's economy and produced record capital investment. Visitors who had not seen North Carolina or studied its economics for awhile could not believe its metamorphosis from America's boondocks to a leader in the technological revolution.

The Research Triangle Park, based in Durham, is the largest university-related research

A youthful entrepreneur makes the best of a downtown flood on Franklin Street in Chapel Hill, circa 1914. Local reformers also made the most of the situation by campaigning for better streets.

enclave in the world, employing more than thirty-five thousand scientists, technicians, and support personnel. A Durham County tax district carved out of pinelands in the 1950s, the park gets its name from its affiliation with the three universities. Research Triangle Park scientists have developed everything from Astroturf to the AIDS-fighting drug AZT. More than seventy research companies, including Glaxo Wellcome and CIBA, a state-funded biotechnology center, and even the U.S. Environmental Protection Agency and the U.S. Forest Service, maintain facilities in the park. Fifteen smaller corporate parks have grown up elsewhere in Durham as well. The result is a steady stream of cars, filled with scientists and white-collar workers, jamming interstate highways 85 and 40 to Durham each morning and afternoon.

Durham is one of the three points of the state's Triangle region (Raleigh and Chapel Hill are the others), which has grown to include six counties and twenty-six separate communities. Loyalist militia cut Cornwallis Road through the area in 1771 to quell a rebellion and local shopkeeper William Johnston forged Revolutionary ammunition and helped underwrite Daniel Boone's explorations into the western mountains. In 1823 Dr. Bartlett Durham, a local physician for whom a tiny town was later named, provided funds for a railroad station. It was in Durham that Confederate General Joseph E. Johnston negotiated the largest surrender of the Civil War, seventeen days after Robert E. Lee relinquished his sword at Appomattox in Virginia. During the ceasefire, Yankee and Rebel troops celebrated with smokes made from brightleaf tobacco, a taste that would soon spawn the huge American Tobacco Company, owned by Washington Duke and his family. Liggett & Myers, R. J. Reynolds, and P. Lorillard were all once American Tobacco subsidiaries, and Durham and the Duke family became synonymous with tobacco.

One of American Tobacco's most famous trademarks was "Bull Durham," a brand of

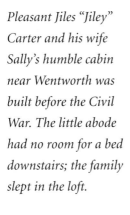

Pleasant Jiles "Jiley" Carter and his wife Sally's humble cabin near Wentworth was built before the Civil War. The little abode had no room for a bed downstairs; the family slept in the loft.

chewing tobacco that spawned such Americanisms as "bullpen" (for a Bull Durham sign in New York's Yankee Stadium) and "shooting the bull" (a not-too-subtle reference to a chewer's aim for the nearest spittoon).

As tobacco factories were joined by denim and hosiery mills, Durham became a raucous boomtown more like the Old West than the Old South. African-Americans shared in the prosperity. Business-man John Merrick founded North Carolina Mutual Life Insurance Company, the largest African-American-owned and managed finan-cial institution in the world, and Durham's Parrish Street became known as America's "Black Wall Street."

The development of Duke University's three campuses, including a huge medical center in 1930—along with the opening of pharma-ceutical research centers, five hospitals, and national diet and fitness centers—contributed to Durham's "City of Medicine, USA" designa-tion. Duke University's Gothic-style chapel, with its 210-foot tower, 5,033-pipe organ, and fifty-bell carillon—and the free, fifty-five-acre Sarah P. Duke Gardens off Campus Drive—have become tourist at-tractions. So have the Duke Homestead and Tobacco Museum and the city's Museum of Life and Science, which houses everything from endangered red wolves to miniature, manmade indoor tornadoes.

The co-author, Carol M. Highsmith, who was born on a farm near Leaksville, North Carolina, enjoys an impish laugh with her older sister Sara in front of her "granny's" Madison home. High-smith recalls helping her older relatives sucker tobacco and pick blackberries.

Once, when there was talk of moving the state capital from Raleigh to Greensboro, a state senator sniggered, "Why, we're not going to leave a thing in Raleigh except the insane asylum, the penitentiary, and the *News and Observer*." Such would hardly be the case today. Owing to the nearby Research Triangle, its own high-tech companies, North Carolina State University in town, and Wake Forest University nearby in Wake County, the "City of Oaks" is home to more Ph.D.'s than any other city in America. The Triangle's largest city is, in the words of one Car-olina writer, "bursting with brainpower." Raleigh also has a restored Victorian neighborhood, an amphitheater that ranks close to the top in the nation in attendance among outdoor con-cert facilities, and the oldest black college in the South—Shaw University, founded in 1865.

"Many folks think of Raleigh as Mayberry [the fictional rural town from the *Andy Griffith* television show], with good ol' Aunt Bea, Sheriff Andy Taylor, and [deputy] Barney," notes the *Raleigh Group Tour Guide*, published by the convention and visitors bureau. "But we're just a little more sophisticated than that!" Raleigh boasts its own African-American Cultural Com-plex, a pocket of museums within a block of the state capitol, a downtown city market, and the state farmers' market. Agribusiness is still North Carolina's leading industry, accounting for about 30 percent of the state's income and 21 percent of its workforce. The Tar Heel State leads the nation in the production of tobacco, turkeys, and sweet potatoes; and is second in hogs, farm-raised trout, and cucumbers made into pickles.

Someone once called Chapel Hill, the third vertex in the Triangle, "the southern part of Heaven," though it's among the least stereotypical of southern towns. University of North Car-olina students from around the nation—and retirees from the world over—give the pleasant little city of 45,000 a vibrant, cosmopolitan flair. One of the best-known landmarks is Sutton's Drugstore, established in 1923, which features one of the last lunch counters still operating in the state. Another popular eatery on Franklin Street is Crook's Corner, which is hard to miss because of the enormous pig on the roof.

Krispy Kreme became a southern institution almost immediately after founder Vernon Rudolph began selling doughnuts hot off the production line at his store in Salem in 1937. A year later, throngs lined up for this opening of his second store in Greensboro.

UNC–Chapel Hill, founded in 1795, is the kingpin of a sixteen-campus statewide system. It was the nation's first state-supported university and the first to admit and graduate students. The university's Old Well, its most famous landmark that is now surrounded by a columned shrine, once served as the college's only water source, giving rise to the campus joke that the only place one could get a bath in Chapel Hill was at the jail. Even though the well's drinking fountain is now tied to the town's water system, the old tradition persists that if UNC freshmen drink from it, they are assured straight A's throughout their collegiate careers. Unfortunately, a glance at most students' grade reports after the first semester refutes the myth.

Two other Orange County communities, Carrboro and Hillsborough, ooze with quaintness. Carrboro, an old railroad and mill town, features a growing arts community and unusual stores and restaurants, including a coffee house and miniature train shop in the old Durham-Greensboro Southern Railway station. Hillsborough, which was laid out on the Great Indian Trading Path, is sometimes called a "museum without walls." It was here that North Carolinians met in a constitutional convention in 1788 to demand that a bill of rights be added to the U.S. Constitution before they would ratify it. More than one hundred late-eighteenth-century and early-nineteenth-century structures still stand here.

North Carolina has a second famous triangle of cities as well. Greensboro, Winston-Salem, and High Point form the "Piedmont Triad." Greensboro, known as the "Gate City" because of its early railroad connections, was the site of that Battle of Guilford Courthouse, one of the most pivotal engagements of the Revolutionary War. British forces won a tactical victory but were so weakened that they surrendered seven months later at Yorktown. The town was then named for General Nathanael Greene, a Revolutionary War hero. Greensboro was an important Civil War

Confederate railroad center, to which President Jefferson Davis fled after the surrender at Appomattox. An exhibit at Greensboro's Historical Museum—located in an 1892 Romanesque church—features recollections of the Union occupation written by William Sidney Porter, under the pen name O. Henry, who lived for a time in Asheville before a bout with "writer's block" prompted him to return to New York. The lives of former First Lady Dolley Madison and legendary broadcaster Edward R. Murrow, who were also Greensboro natives, are also showcased at the museum.

Greensboro's cultural center at Festival Park features an eclectic mix of five galleries, and the city offers a restored 1927 vaudeville theater, the Carolina, where plays, dances, concerts and classic films are now presented. It is also the home of one of the nation's oldest dinner theaters, the Barn Dance Theatre. Greensboro is also noted for its arboretum, bicentennial gardens, and "Bog Garden," which features a half-mile elevated walkway over plants and wildlife.

North of town are a remarkable old, working gristmill at Guilford and the lavish Chinqua-Penn Plantation home, a twenty-seven-room estate in Reidsville. It is full of incredible artifacts from the world travels of its owners, Thomas Jefferson Penn and his wife Margaret. South of Greensboro, in the little crossroads town of Randleman, is the Richard Petty Museum, which includes race cars, trophies, and films of the seven-time Winston Cup Series auto-racing champion.

High Point, which calls itself the "Furnishings Capital of the World," is easily identified by a downtown building painted from top to bottom to look like a chest of drawers. Furniture manufacturing began here in the late 1800s because of the availability of hardwood lumber from the Piedmont's virgin forests and the proximity of eastern population centers. The city, which is full of furniture factories and outlet shops—many of which are small and family-owned— hosts the International Home Furnishings Market twice a year, to which more than seventy thousand visitors repair in search of ideas and bargains. High Point's Furniture Discovery Center explains the intricate steps involved in making both cabinets and upholstered furniture.

Winston-Salem, on the western edge of the Triad, was founded as Salem by German Moravians in 1766. It was both a pious missionary outpost and a rowdy frontier supply depot. The inventory of barrels, kitchenware, woodwork, and handwoven clothes at the nonprofit, restored Old Salem village is testament to the town's mercantile past. With its working bakery, shoemaker's shop, Single Brothers' House, restored private homes, and the Salem Tavern (where sauerkraut stew and deviled duck are still on the menu), Old Salem hies to a standard of authentic, even academic, restoration, rather than turning its buildings into "adaptive re-use" visitor centers or gift shops. Old Salem offers horticultural "vignettes," including stone yards, cultivated terrace gardens, and rows of fruit bushes and trees.

The modern town of Winston, which was combined with Salem in 1913, was built as a tobacco, furniture, and textile center. Its R. J. Reynolds Tobacco Company still turns leaves into cigarettes and offers free guided tours. In one corner of town stands the Reynolda House Museum of American Art, built in 1917 as the manse on the model farm of tobacco magnate Richard Joshua Reynolds and his wife Katharine. Displayed there are three centuries of important American

Settlers Charlotte and Timothy Vogler catch a breeze on their stoop in Salem, about 1895. Vogler, a gunsmith for more than fifty years, ran the Salem Tavern for a time in the old Moravian settlement.

paintings, prints, and sculptures, and Katharine Smith Reynolds's magnificent formal gardens.

Not far west of Winston-Salem—but much higher in altitude—in the heart of the Blue Ridge Mountains, is the college town of Boone, home of fast-growing Appalachian State University. Boone—named for the explorer who blazed a wilderness road on his way to Kentucky's "dark and bloody ground"—could steal a page from Denver and call itself "The Kilometer-High City." It is a stop on the meandering Blue Ridge Parkway, which stretches 469 scenic, ridge-top miles from western Virginia to the Great Smoky Mountain National Park in Tennessee. So rugged was the North Carolina high country that, as late as 1825, the area that would become Avery County had just thirteen families—one for every nineteen square miles. Today, Boone and its surroundings are a magnet for fall "leaf peepers," and the surrounding area is filled with natural wonders, including Grandfather Mountain—the highest peak in the Blue Ridge Mountains. Wealthy planters from throughout the lowland South agreed with Boone's slogan—"The Coolest Spot in the South"—as they built many cottages in the area to escape the summer heat.

The largest city in the Carolina mountains is Asheville, where the Great Smokies and the Blue Ridge Mountains meet. It's a surprising place with more Art Deco architecture than any other southeastern city save Miami Beach. The nation's preeminent organization representing the crafts culture of the southern Appalachians, the Southern Highland Handicraft Guild, was founded in Asheville in 1930. The guild is based at milepost 382 on the Blue Ridge Parkway, where members' works are displayed and sold. Asheville is a lively festival city; more than two hundred mountain jamborees are held in town and surrounding communities each year.

Once a resort and rehabilitation town frequented by thousands of "summer people" each year, Asheville, more than any other American city, was devastated by the Stock Market Crash of

Folks at the original Mast General Store, founded in 1883 in Valle Crucis, near Boone, say that the only thing that changes there is the paint. For a look inside today, see page 104.

1929. That's because the city government chose to pay back every dollar it lost when the big Central Bank and Trust Company folded—an obligation that would take forty-seven years to fulfill. But there was a bright side: because the city was so poor, it could not afford to tear down old buildings and embark upon urban renewal. The result is a stock of remarkably preserved buildings, including the flashy Art Deco city hall. Somewhere in Asheville's first skyscraper, erected in 1924, an obscure draftsman named Walt Disney was fired for daydreaming and doodling!

Tucked among the more than one million acres of national forestland that surround Asheville is a Victorian treasure that took a thousand men more than five years to complete. It's the 225-room Biltmore Estate, once the chateau of art collectors and world travelers George and Edith Vanderbilt and the largest private residence in North America. Here more than fifty thousand artworks, furnishings, and antiques are exhibited. Almost since George Washington Vanderbilt's purchase of the 125,000 acres of farms, woods, and forested hillsides at the turn of the century, historic preservation of the estate, winery, and Frederick Law Olmsted's English walled garden has been a never-ending process. One year, for instance, the staff concentrated on the estate's sixteenth-century Flemish tapestries. Another time, it was the library's paneled ceiling, which a conservation team from England carefully removed, cleaned, and reinstalled. To accommodate the curiosity of guests who wonder about the off-limits "back of the house," Biltmore curators even offer behind-the-scenes tours of rooms such as Mrs. Vanderbilt's maid's quarters, a sewing room, and the subbasement.

About one thousand Cherokee Indians in North Carolina and Tennessee escaped the roundup and forced relocation of their people along the "Trail of Tears" to Oklahoma in the 1830s. Eventually they gained recognition as an Indian nation—the Eastern Band of Cherokees.

The East Tennessee & Western North Carolina Railroad— or "Tweetsie" line as it was affectionately known—ran through the rugged Blue Ridge chain of the Appalachian Mountains, beginning in 1881. This is the Cranberry, North Carolina, depot in 1946.

About ten thousand Cherokees live today on a fifty-six-thousand-acre reservation that they call the Qualla Boundary, with tribal headquarters in the mountain town of Cherokee, west of Asheville. Here, visitors find the Museum of the Cherokee Indian, a casino, campgrounds, and some of the nation's best trout fishing in regularly stocked streams. On summer nights at an outdoor mountainside theater, Cherokees perform in *Unto These Hills*, a drama about their people's tormented history. Cherokee is also one of the few places in the eastern United States where one can have a picture taken with a Native American on Indian-owned land—usually in return for a fee or tip.

Heading east and slightly south out of the mountains, the terrain falls sharply from peaks of six thousand feet to an elevation under eight hundred feet around Charlotte, the Carolinas' largest city at just under five hundred thousand in population. It is a place for which the word "dynamic" was intended. The city has a restless, relentless beat. "Charlotte achieves its meaning primarily from what it aspires to be, not what it's been," UNC–Charlotte history professor Dan Morrill told the *New York Times*. The "Queen City's" tidy downtown is packed with shiny skyscrapers and an astounding array of public art, much of it corporately funded. Four of the sculptures, including the figure of a mother holding her baby aloft to represent the future, were erected on the corners of a single downtown intersection.

So explosive has been the growth of banking, including the acquisition by Charlotte-based banks of other regional banking goliaths on both sides of the Mississippi River, that the city is now the nation's second-largest financial center, behind New York. Charlotte is still agog over its acquisition, in the early 1990s, of a National Football League franchise, the Panthers, for whom the city and Mecklenburg County, as well as franchise owner Jerry Richardson and other investors, built a state-of-the-art, seventy-two-thousand-seat stadium on the edge of the central business district. Charlotte is also a major-league basketball city and home to one of stock-car racing's shrines, the Charlotte Motor Speedway. The Coca-Cola 600 race held here each year is the nation's second-largest spectator sporting event in attendance, second only to another auto race, the Indianapolis 500.

Romantic and satiric novelist Thomas Wolfe poses with his mother, Julia, outside the family's boarding house in Asheville in 1937. Wolfe died young, at age 37. Thomas Wolfe's Letters to His Mother *was published posthumously in 1943.*

One of three kinds of attire would put one right at home during a drive through the southeastern lowlands of North Carolina: golfing togs, for the area boasts some of the nation's most beautiful and highest-rated courses; a woodsman's outfit for use in the widespread pine forests; or a military uniform. Two gigantic military preserves are fixtures in the area: the Army's Fort Bragg, home to the 82d Airborne paratroop division and Special Forces "Green Berets," between Southern Pines and Fayetteville; and the Marine Corps' "boot camp" at Camp Lejeune near Jacksonville. Additionally, the big Seymour Johnson Air Force Base near Goldsboro is not far away.

This is plantation and battlefield country as well. At Orton Plantation and Gardens south of Wilmington, Poplar Grove just north of downtown, and elsewhere in southeastern North Carolina, the wealth of merchants, planters, and shipping interests brought beautiful homes, gracious lifestyles, and cultural amenities to the region.

The seductively charming old port and shipbuilding city of Wilmington boasts a two-hundred-block historic district, the largest registered in the state. Among sites of interest are the Bellamy Mansion

and Thalian Hall theater, opened in 1858, where "Buffalo Bill" Cody, Lillian Russell, and John Philip Sousa all performed. The state's largest city was left isolated and withering on poor two-lane roads when interstate highways joined the Triad and Triangle but went nowhere near the old cotton, lumber, and tar port. Now the terminus of Interstate 40, Wilmington is enjoying a renaissance. Heavily fortified during the Civil War, it was the last Atlantic Coast Confederate port to remain open to trade. Only after a massive naval bombardment, during which fifty Union warships pounded Fort Fisher for forty-eight straight hours, did Wilmington finally fall to occupying forces. This was the world's largest land-sea battle until D-Day during World War II. Today, one of North Carolina's three state aquariums is located at Fort Fisher, and a battleship from another war, the USS *North Carolina*, which spent forty months in World War II combat, is berthed and open to tours in Wilmington's harbor. The ship's main batteries once fired shells weighing as much as a midsize car a distance of twenty miles.

Tryon Palace is the building considered the most beautiful in colonial America. A royal mansion that became North Carolina's first capitol, it is the centerpiece of another historic river town, New Bern. Founded by Swiss and German settlers on a peninsula at the confluence of the Neuse and Trent rivers in 1710, picturesque New Bern retains a languid pace unusual in this energetic state. At Tryon Palace, ladies in silk and gentlemen in powdered wigs once danced by candlelight as the guests of Royal Governor William Tryon. Later, North Carolina's first state governor, Richard Caswell, entertained there as well. The original palace burned in 1798; it was reconstructed from English architect John Hawk's original plans on a different downtown site in the 1950s.

Today New Bern's shops are loaded with "bear necessities"—stuffed bears, toy bears, and

Inveterate world traveler and art collector George W. Vanderbilt decorated each of the 225 rooms in his Biltmore House, near Asheville. Each year, the Biltmore staff restores a few rooms.

Golf was an afterthought at the Pinehurst Resort, built by Bostonian James Walker Tufts and landscaped by Frederick Law Olmsted. Until an early guest brought golf clubs, members and guests mainly played tennis, polo, and croquet. By 1897 players were hitting balls around the dairy pasture.

books on bears. That's because the city borrowed the heraldic symbol—emblazoned with an ursine figure—of its namesake city in Switzerland. "Bern" is the old Germanic word for bear. New Bern calls itself North Carolina's "City of Firsts," for good reason. For example, Pepsi-Cola, originally called "Brad's Drink" after its inventor, pharmacist Caleb Bradham, was perfected here. New Bern saw North Carolina's first printing press, postal service, motion picture theater, and outdoor Christmas lights. And it was the first city in America to celebrate George Washington's birthday.

Up the coast in the state's northeastern corner are the Outer Banks, the state's favorite beach resort and the site, at Kill Devil Hills, where the Wright Brothers, after four years of trying, succeeded in launching history's first powered flight on December 17, 1903. Hang gliding is more the rage today over the twenty-eight thousand acres of America's first National Seashore. The highest sand dunes on the East Coast can be found at Jockey's Ridge State Park, and on the west side of the long sandbars are several sounds that comprise the third-largest estuary system in the world. Near Manteo on Roanoke Island, the roots of English America are remembered at the restored earthworks and museum at Fort Raleigh National Historic Site. The *Elizabeth II*, a period replica named after one of the ships that brought the first settlers to Roanoke Island, is berthed in Manteo harbor as well. There's a second state aquarium nearby, and a theater where the nation's oldest outdoor drama, *The Lost Colony*, is presented with symphonic accompaniment each summer. Andy Griffith is one of many actors who got their first breaks performing in the spectacle. The Outer Banks are also full of art galleries, wildlife refuges and birding spots, lighthouses, crisscrossing ferries, and windsurfers' inlets.

There is one more "must-see" North Carolina stop for nature lovers. It's a six-hundred-

square-mile swamp that overlaps the border between northeastern North Carolina and Virginia. In 1728, Colonel William Byrd II of Virginia led a surveying expedition into the swamp in an effort to establish the dividing line between the two states. His men were nearly devoured by yellow flies, chiggers, mosquitoes, and ticks. Byrd was the first to name the swamp "Dismal"—a "vast body of dirt and nastiness." In May 1763, George Washington visited the swamp and suggested draining it and building a north-south canal to connect the waters of the Chesapeake Bay and Albemarle Sound. Various ditches were dug, and huge tracts of juniper, gum, cedar, and cypress trees were harvested. Long after Washington died, a canal connecting the Elizabeth River in Virginia and the Pasquotank River in North Carolina was completed. The oldest surviving manmade waterway in the United States is now part of the U.S. Army Corps of Engineers' great Atlantic Intracoastal Waterway and is enjoyed mainly by pleasure boaters. (Commercial vessels by and large use the newer, parallel Albemarle & Chesapeake Canal.) A big paper company bought the surrounding land and harvested the remaining original timber, then donated the land to the Nature Conservancy, which in turn deeded it to the federal government to create the Great Dismal Swamp National Wildlife Refuge.

In *The Book of America*, their 1983 study of the fifty states, Neal R. Peirce and Jerry Hagstrom called North Carolina "the newest megastate." Often overshadowed by courtly Virginia, enterprising Georgia, electrifying Florida, and eccentric Louisiana—and lacking a single magnet city like Atlanta—North Carolina snuck up on the nation's consciousness. What it reveals when people discover it is a diverse land of pleasant cities, majestic mountains, caressing beach breezes, and bursts of history that seem to pop from behind every pine tree. A megastate it is, but North Carolina has never let loose of its down-home culture, cuisine, and character.

Jockey's Ridge State Park (left), north of Nags Head, boasts the tallest natural sand dune in the East. Its height fluctuates between one hundred and one hundred twenty feet. Resisting development, local residents persuaded the state to establish the park in 1975. Although the origin of its name is a mystery, mustang races were once held at the base of the dune as spectators watched from above. The eighty-ton Wright Brothers National Memorial (above), carved from solid North Carolina granite, crowns Big Kill Devil Hill, a once-shifting ninety-foot dune that has been stabilized with grass by the U.S. Army Corps of Engineers. The sixty-foot pylon marks the site of the hundreds of glider flights that preceded the Wrights' first powered flight.

At 208 feet, the 1870 Cape Hatteras Lighthouse (opposite) at Buxton on the Outer Banks is the tallest brick lighthouse in America. Its former keeper's residence serves as a welcome center, and visitors may climb the lighthouse's 268 steps for a spectacular view of the national seashore. The light station was essential, for more than six hundred ships are known to have been wrecked on the shallow shoals offshore in the "Graveyard of the Atlantic." Elizabeth II (above), moored in Manteo harbor, the birthplace of English America, is a sixty-nine-foot square-rigged sailing vessel similar in design to the sixteenth-century ship that brought England's first colonists to Roanoke Island. Aboard, costumed interpreters describe the three-month visit to the New World. Nearby, the Garden Club of North Carolina has created the sixteenth-century-style Elizabethan Gardens as a living memorial to these "lost colonists," who disappeared without a trace.

Private ferry service connecting North Carolina coastal points like Cedar Island, Cherry Branch, Hatteras, Ocracoke, Fort Fisher, and Currituck began in the 1920s. In 1934 the state began subsidizing the service, and in 1947 it began its own system, now one of the nation's largest. Small free ferries and large toll ferries—painted with the colors and emblems of the state universities—operate year-round. This vessel (above) represents the University of North Carolina–Charlotte. Shrimp and crab boats like the Miss Melissa (opposite), plus excursion boats and an extensive charter fishing fleet, ply the same waters. According to the International Gamefish Association, the Outer Banks and the Virgin Islands are the most likely places to catch an Atlantic blue marlin, which can weigh more than one thousand pounds. Several Hatteras restaurants will clean and cook visitors' catches— of whatever species— for a nominal fee.

Without "snow" fences (opposite), dunes on the Outer Banks would shift dangerously, as only the hardiest of grasses can get a foothold. Surf fishing is popular along the shore, as is leisurely casting from the Hatteras pier (top left). Beach cottage owners need not create a "weathered look" for their properties; howling Atlantic storms do the job (bottom left). Developable land is scarce, because the Cape Hatteras National Seashore occupies much of the Outer Banks. The mysterious Great Dismal Swamp (overleaf) connects North Carolina's Albemarle Sound to the Chesapeake Bay in Virginia via an old canal and the modern Atlantic Intracoastal Waterway. George Washington, who suggested the canal, formed a syndicate that tried, unsuccessfully, to drain the Dismal Swamp. The company cut most of the swamp's cypress trees for shingles and shipbuilding.

The Newbold-White House (left), built circa 1730 in Perquimans County, is North Carolina's oldest known brick house. Filled with period furnishings, it is open to the public. Buried on the grounds is Philip Ludwell, first governor (1689–91) of the part of Carolina lying north and east of the Cape Fear River. The world's only Country Doctor Museum (above) in Bailey, east of Raleigh, was chartered in 1967 by two female physicians, "country doctor" Josephine Newell and dermatologist Gloria Graham. The museum is a composite restoration of two nineteenth-century offices, including examining rooms and an apothecary. Visitors see such items as bleeding bowls, Victorian inhalers, and an old operating table. Most medical instruments dating to the 1880s, as well as other exhibits, were donated by area physicians and interested citizens.

Travel & Leisure magazine called Edenton (above) "the South's prettiest town." Here, observed the article's author, "antebellum" does not refer to the period before the Civil War; it means pre-Revolution. Once a prosperous seaport on Albemarle Sound, Edenton today is a languorous showplace for crape myrtles, magnolias and giant elms, and both annual and perennial flowers. A number of pre-Revolution houses are now publicly owned by Historic Edenton, Inc. Jet-skiers and pleasure boaters use Pembroke Creek (right) to access the sound. In another historic community, New Bern, Tryon Palace (overleaf) was the meeting place of the North Carolina colonial assembly and the residence of British Royal Governor William Tryon. After the Revolution, state governors lived there, and guest George Washington danced in its great ballroom.

New Bern—North Carolina's second-oldest town and its first capital—boasts more than 150 historic landmarks, including hundreds of immaculately maintained or restored old homes like these dwellings (left) on Craven Street. Several date to the Civil War, when New Bern was a Union-controlled city in Confederate territory. The circa-1883 Second Empire-style Craven County Courthouse (above) features a unique mansard roof with patterned, colored slates. On the lawn is the "Governors' Boulder," containing bronze tablets honoring three governors from New Bern. In a delightful coincidence, one of the city's finest restored homes, the Harvey Mansion, is now owned and operated as a fine restaurant by Chef Beat Zuttel and his wife, Carolyn. Zuttel is from the city's namesake city, Bern, Switzerland.

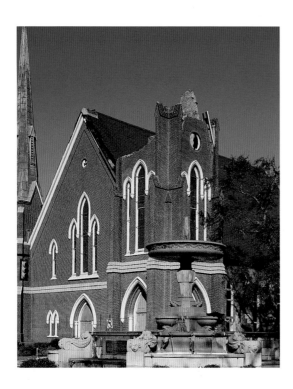

The Bellamy Mansion (right) is one of beautiful Wilmington's most spectacular examples of antebellum architecture. Its builder, planter John D. Bellamy, and his family were displaced by Union forces but reclaimed the house after the Civil War. The building, which is now the property of Preservation North Carolina and a museum, features tours and changing exhibitions on the sultry old city's history and design arts. Even though the steeple of Wilmington's First Baptist Church (above) had been reinforced to withstand hurricanes, it toppled in a 1996 storm. The Atlantic Intracoastal Highway (overleaf), a protected water route from Norfolk, Virginia, to Key West, Florida, passes through Wilmington.

Polly Slocum, the "Heroic Woman of the Lower Cape Fear," is remembered with a statue (above) on the Moores Creek Battlefield in Currie. Wife of Lieutenant Ezekiel Slocum, a Revolutionary War patriot, she is reputed to have ridden alone sixty-five miles at night to succor the wounded at the battle that ended royal authority in North Carolina Colony. Southern North Carolina is largely rural, with isolated farms and simple cabins (left). Late at night, one can often drive without seeing lights of homes or passing cars. Near the settlement of Coats (overleaf), tobacco flowers bloom. The blossoms will be "topped"—removed— enhancing leaf weight and aroma.

The 1905 Union Station (above) in the little town of Aberdeen, near Southern Pines, was an old Seaboard Coast Line and Norfolk Southern station when those railroads connected North Carolina with cities in Florida. The caboose is from the old Aberdeen and Rockfish Railroad that carried freight and pine logs to Fayetteville. Pinehurst Resort (right), since its founding in 1895, has been a magnet for golfers. Scotsman Donald Ross designed four courses at the club—and three others in the Pinehurst area—in the early 1900s. Ben Hogan won his first professional tournament in 1940 at the resort, and Pinehurst has been a U.S. Open site and a regular PGA Tour stop.

Since 1986, the First North Carolina Volunteers, a Civil War re-enactment organization, has staged an annual fullscale "battle" at Fort Branch, near Hamilton. Confederate forces (left) pass the time beside their campfire. Fort Branch, which protected "the Lifeline of the Confederacy"—a railroad bridge that helped supply General Robert E. Lee's army with provisions—was never taken by Union forces. One of the state's delightful and eccentric attractions is Mary and Marvin Johnson's Gourd Museum (above) at Kennebec, north of Angier. A farmer and mathematics teacher, Marvin Johnson grew, decorated, carved, and collected gourds and objects made from gourds. Friends and visitors added to the collection, which now contains more that one thousand specimens.

North Carolina's 1891 governor's mansion (above) is a Queen Anne-style brick structure with gingerbread trim. On Fayetteville Street stands Bruno Lucchesi's 1976 statue of Sir Walter Raleigh (opposite), for whom the capital city is named. Raleigh is often thought to have "discovered" North Carolina, but he never left the Old World. From London, he sent forth the expeditions that founded the first English colony in America. His namesake city is the only state capital to have been established on land specifically purchased by a state for its government seat. Today the "City of Oaks"—home to North Carolina State University and a cornerstone of the state's Research Triangle—is bursting with brainpower. It is said to be home to more Ph.D.'s than any other U.S. city.

Charles Keck executed the statue (opposite) on the North Carolina Capitol grounds that honors three North Carolinians who became U.S. presidents: James Polk, born near Pineville, was an expansionist who led the nation into the Mexican War; Andrew Johnson, born in Raleigh, who became president upon Abraham Lincoln's assassination, was impeached by the House of Representatives but found "not guilty" by the Senate; and Andrew Jackson, "Old Hickory," who may not have been born in North Carolina at all! North and South Carolina each maintains that Jackson's mother delivered the future president in its territory—the boundary and her exact whereabouts are now uncertain. Neither state has conclusively proved its case. North Carolina Confederate officers and soldiers are buried in several honored sections of Raleigh's Oakwood Cemetery (left).

Oakwood, Raleigh's first local historic district, is a neighborhood of Victorian homes (right) covering twenty downtown blocks. Most were built just after the Civil War in dense woods known as "Mordecai Grove." Many of the largest homes have been subdivided into apartments. The North Carolina Department of Agriculture operates a huge farmers' market (above) in Raleigh. In all seasons, its eleven buildings offer wholesale and retail fruits, vegetables, seafood, and ornamental plants, a full-service restaurant and a separate seafood eatery. North Carolina leads the nation in the production of tobacco, sweet potatoes, and turkeys, and is second in hogs, cucumber pickles, and—of all things— trout! Other crops not often associated with North Carolina but in which the state is a top-four producer are grapes, catfish, and sweet corn.

Patterson's Mill Country Store (left), modeled after the original Patterson & Co. emporium of the 1870s, has been open in Durham County since 1973. The rambling store building houses a furnished early twentieth-century doctor's office; artifacts from the old Patterson's Mill community; a vintage collection of general store items; and regional crafts, antiques, and collectibles for sale. The chapel tower (above) remains the focal point of Duke University's Durham campus. (For a vintage view of the chapel, see page 8.) The fifty-five-acre Sarah P. Duke Gardens (overleaf) on the university's West Campus include terraces, waterfalls, an Asiatic arboretum, and five miles of allées, walks, and pathways.

The Museum of Life and Science in Durham is full of surprises, inside and out. Exhibits have included an actual Piedmont Airlines DC-3 (left) in the picnic area and a Magic Wings butterfly enclosure in a lush botanical garden (above). Among visitors' scientific adventures at the museum: studying geologic formations—including Oregon's Mount Saint Helens after it erupted—in the "Data Earth" section; pressing nose to glass at the river otter tank at "Carolina Wildlife"; interacting with the science behind medicine at "BodyTech"; watching tornadoes form in the weather exhibit; and observing endangered red wolves in the woodland habitat. There are also chemistry, biology, and children's labs open to the public. The museum has served eastern and central North Carolina since 1946.

The 167-foot bell tower (opposite) on the University of North Carolina campus in Chapel Hill was designed by New York architects McKim, Mead, and White in 1931. The red brick and Indiana limestone tower was the gift of the Morehead and Patterson families, whose members had been teachers, students, and trustees of the university. The tower features a nine-foot clock face on each of its four sides, and twelve bells, ranging in weight from three hundred to thirty-five hundred pounds. The Old Well (above) has been the unofficial symbol of the Chapel Hill campus. For many years it served as the sole supply for the Old East and Old West dormitories, which gave rise to the campus joke that the only place one could get a bath was in jail. Once a plain wooden structure, the well was beautified in 1897.

Wilsie (above) is more than an Ayrshire dairy cow. She's also a free-roaming pet on Lewis Cheek's farm near Calvander. Cheek sits astride his tractor (opposite) on the two-hundred-acre spread. The bins behind him contain carefully mixed bulk feed for milk cows in the right bin, heifers in the center container, and calves in the left bin. Only Wisconsin, California, and New York State produce more milk than North Carolina—which delivers more than 1.5 billion pounds a year. (The measure is in pounds rather than gallons because that's how farmers are paid— by the hundred pounds of milk delivered.) The Tar Heel State, with more than 1.2 million cattle on farms, ranks fourth in that category. To feed livestock, hay rolls like those on a farm along old North Carolina Highway 86 outside Hillsborough (overleaf) are put away for the winter.

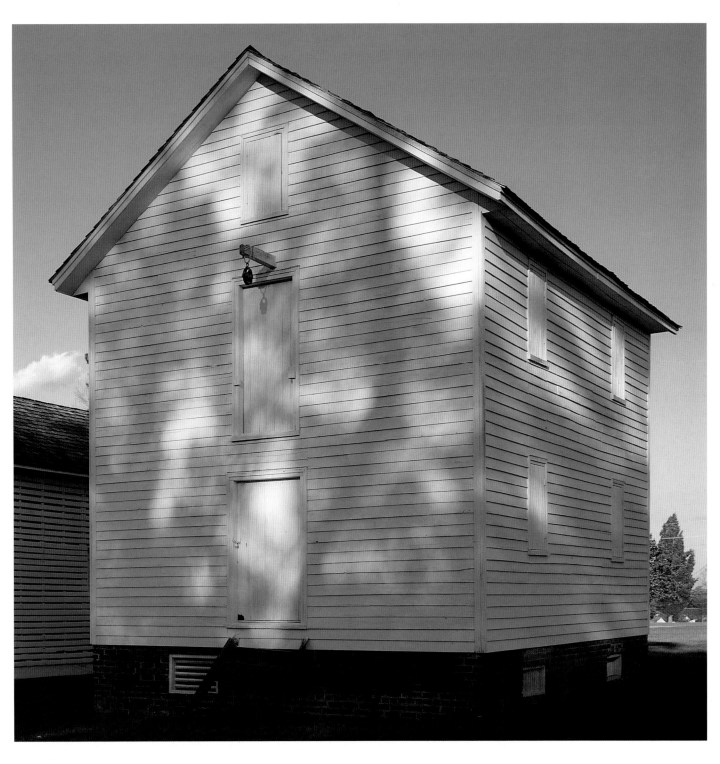

Chinqua-Penn mansion (opposite) near Reidsville was built in 1925 by inveterate world travelers Thomas Jefferson "Jeff" Penn and his wife Betsy. The manor's name derives from the family surname and the chinquapin, a dwarf chestnut tree that abounded on the estate. The Penns decorated their lavish, twenty-seven-room home with furnishings gathered in Russia, China, Egypt, France, and beyond, and the collection presents North Carolina's most eclectic examples of Oriental and religious art. Eventually placed under the stewardship of the state university system, Chinqua-Penn was forced to close in 1991 because of reductions in state appropriations. It has since reopened under the auspices of a nonprofit foundation. A beautifully restored granary and a corn crib (above) were constructed on the Alamance County plantation of Edwin Holt, a southern textile industry pioneer, in 1874. The estate is now the Alamance County Historical Museum.

Binford "Benny" Carter Jr. (right) of Rockingham County is a former grocery store and aluminum fabrication company employee who has become one of the nation's hottest folk artists. His offbeat paintings of New York City and San Francisco are in demand worldwide. The Charlotte Observer wrote that Carter, who collects other artists' birdhouses and airplane sculptures, is a "country boy with a New York City vision." A beautiful 1910 three-row Denzel Menagerie carousel (opposite) has become the symbol of the textile city of Burlington. In addition to its twenty-six horses, it features four each of cats, ostriches, rabbits, and pigs; two chariots; and one deer, giraffe, lion, and tiger. Each September, Burlington hosts a Carousel Festival, attracting national artists who specialize in creating paintings for these colorful merry-go-rounds.

Rockingham County farmer William "Doot" Vernon paid a visit (opposite) to his neighbor, Kate Carter, in the mid-1980s. Both they and Mrs. Carter's barn are gone now. Rural cabins, many with rusting tin roofs (top left) are becoming a less common sight in rapidly modernizing North Carolina. These cabins were the subject of Elizabeth Edwards's painting on page 7. For more years than anyone can remember, the Carter clan of North Carolina has held reunions on the family farm near Wentworth. Carters come from as far away as Minnesota, but the food is pure southern (and delicious): green beans with fatback, soggy tomato sandwiches, a dozen kinds of fried chicken, turnip greens and black-eyed peas, deviled eggs, watermelon, and fried pies.

Reynolda House in Winston-Salem was once the gracious country home of Richard Joshua Reynolds, founder of the R. J. Reynolds Tobacco Company, and his wife Katharine. It is now a nonprofit museum of American art. Above the marble fireplace in the formal dining room (above) is Martin Johnson Heade's 1871 Brazilian scene, Orchid with Two Hummingbirds. The furniture represents the collections of two generations of Reynoldses; the silver was a fourth anniversary present from Richard to Katharine. Landscaping is central to the restoration of Old Salem, where gardens (opposite) were an extension of Moravian households. That restoration has been scrupulously faithful to the authentic nineteenth-century village. Out went golf-course-quality greens in favor of horticultural "vignettes"—stone yards, cultivated terraced gardens, and rows of fruit bushes and trees. Beehives are tended, compost piles maintained, and rye and tobacco are harvested.

In downtown Greensboro, there's a statue to native William Sidney Porter (above) who entertained millions of readers with his short stories at the turn of the century. He adopted the pen name "O. Henry" while serving time at a federal penitentiary for embezzling funds from a Texas bank. In Oak Ridge in Guilford County stands the Old Mill of Guilford (right), built in the 1760s. Charles Parnell, who bought and renovated the mill in 1977, still grinds grain there for pancake mix and other uses. Wildflowers (overleaf) sown in one of the nation's most ambitious highway beautification programs make nearby U.S. Highway 29 and other roads throughout the state visually appealing.

At the Furniture Discovery Center (above) in a renovated fabric warehouse in High Point, visitors can get a walk-through of the furniture-making process, from the cutting of trees to the making of a frame, to the gluing and application of veneer, stains, and polishes. Each April and October, when buyers descend on High Point for the semiannual wholesale furniture market, visitors from more than eighty-five countries tour the discovery center. In the same building is the Angela Peterson Doll and Miniature Museum (opposite), featuring more than seventeen hundred dolls, miniatures, and artifacts collected by Mrs. Peterson during a lifetime of world travel. "I never bought a doll I didn't like," she once said, "and never sold a doll after it was mine." Among the miniatures displayed are three couples of fully dressed "fleas" that must be viewed under a magnifier.

Charlotte exhibits an amazing array of public art, including this Gold Miner Statue (above) representing Commerce. (Charlotte was the site of the nation's first gold rush.) The miner is one of four Raymond Kaskey statues commissioned by the Queen's Table, a group of art lovers, for the four corners of The Square uptown. The others represent Industry, Transportation, and the Future. In the mid-1800s, Charlotte was divided into four political wards. Some of the most beautiful remaining homes from that period are found in the Fourth Ward (right), which for a time was neglected but now is so fashionable that half its houses, saved from demolition in other parts of town, were moved there.

Bunker Hill Covered Bridge (left) across Lyle's Creek on Old Island Ford Road in Catawba County was erected in 1894. It was restored by the county historical association in 1994. Although cotton takes a back seat to tobacco in the Tar Heel State, fields of the fiber (above) abound in the south-central part of the state. Only Texas, California, and Georgia produce more bales than North Carolina. The pointed cotton fruit—the boll, from which the destructive insect, the boll weevil, gets its name—is tightly closed until it matures. Then it opens to reveal fluffy fibers just before harvest. After leaves have been removed by defoliation using chemical sprays, most ripe cotton plants are gathered today not by hand, but by mechanical strippers.

The Latta Plantation (right) in Huntersville, north of Charlotte, is the last remaining Catawba River plantation open to the public. Its original owner, Scots-Irish immigrant James Latta, was a traveling merchant who purchased wares in Philadelphia and Charleston and sold them in backwater Carolina counties. Settling in Mecklenburg County, Latta and his family prospered, growing cotton on 742 acres and building a two-story Federalist-style home. As many as thirty-two slaves did the work—cooking, washing, spinning, planting, plowing, harvesting, and tending to livestock. The grounds include several outbuildings (above), some moved from other rural piedmont farms. On many of those farms, buildings included barns like this one in Watauga County (overleaf), where blend tobacco was—and is to this day—air cured.

The pot-bellied stove still works at the Mast General Store (above) in Valle Crucis, where Kenneth Townsend, left, and Howell Cook engage in a good-natured game of checkers using bottle caps from old-fashioned sodas still sold at the store. Valle Crucis, Spanish for "Vale of the Cross," got its name from Episcopal missionaries; two valleys cross at this settlement in this high country near Boone. The store opened in 1883. W. W. Mast, who bought it in 1897, said he always attempted to stock everything his neighbors might need, from "cradles to caskets." Toward the back is a "chicken hatch," a trap door where Mast deposited chickens that he had accepted in trade for merchandise. Behind the store is the town's 1907 schoolhouse. North Carolina is rich with country scenes, including this old wagon (opposite) outside another general store in Catawba.

The Grassy Knob Tunnel (above) thrusts the Blue Ridge Parkway through a mountainside near Sleepy Gap in western North Carolina. The 469-mile parkway follows mountain crests from Shenandoah National Park in Virginia to Smoky Mountains National Park in North Carolina and Tennessee. The serpentine drive is slow but scenic, with numerous spectacular overlooks (right). The Blue Ridge Parkway Association, comprised of more than seven hundred businesses and attractions, is headquartered in Asheville. Along an old road through Maggie Valley lined with craft shops, pancake houses, and small zoos, a mountain storm (overleaf) roils in the distance. The mountains from Cherokee to Boone are the coolest spot in the South, with average summertime temperatures of sixty-nine degrees and plenty of winter snow for skiing.

The mountain town of Cherokee, in far-western North Carolina, anchors the reservation of the Cherokee Nation—part of its ancestral home that stretches over parts of what are now eight states from Virginia to Alabama. The town is full of gift shops and trading posts (opposite). Peter Wolf Toth carved the statue of the great Cherokee leader Sequoyah (left) out of a giant Northwest sequoia, donated and shipped by the Georgia Pacific Company in 1989. The statue stands outside the Museum of the Cherokee Indian, which, in part, tells of the terrible "Trail of Tears" forced evacuation of Cherokees to Oklahoma's "Indian Territory." Today, Dennis Wolfe (above), a full-blooded Cherokee, is one of several Native Americans willing to pose for visitors.

Some of North Carolina's most beautiful settings, including Lake Junaluska (right) and the Hawk Creek Valley (overleaf) dot the western hills around Asheville and Black Mountain. In Flat Rock, Carl Sandburg and his wife Paula lived on a farm called Connemara (opposite). For twenty-two years beginning in 1945, Sandburg—the legendary poet, author, lecturer, minstrel, and biographer of Abraham Lincoln—consulted his library of more than ten thousand volumes moved from the family's previous home in Michigan, and delighted in the farm's splendid isolation. At Connemara, Sandburg wrote his autobiography, Always the Young Strangers, *as well as his only novel,* Remembrance Rock, *which traced the American saga from Plymouth Rock to World War II. Mrs. Sandburg ran the farm and tended to her prize-winning goat herd.*

Begun as a frontier outpost in 1797, Asheville was originally little more than a crossroads of Indian trails on a plateau, surrounded by imposing mountains. It later became a resort town for therapeutic health treatments, then a railroad center, and then a mecca for southern "summer people" seeking an escape from the steamy heat. The city soon became an architectural laboratory. Structures such as City Hall (above) are part of a southeastern Art Deco inventory second only to that of Miami Beach. Thomas Wolfe's Queen Anne-style boyhood home (opposite) was his mother's boarding house, called "Old Kentucky Home," after which he modeled Eliza Gant's "Dixieland" in his first novel, Look Homeward, Angel. In it, he remembered the structure as a "big cheaply constructed frame house of eighteen or twenty drafty, high-ceilinged rooms." The house is now a North Carolina Historic Site.

Asheville's 1926 First Baptist Church (above) was designed by North Carolinian Douglas Ellington, a master of Art Deco. Ellington employed a gradation of colored mission tiles on the dome; and orange bricks, terra cotta moldings, and pink marble on the walls. A streetcorner in downtown Asheville (opposite) reveals a variety of forms and functions: lamppost, fountain, horse's head, and street sculpture of a young girl. The region's best-known address is the Biltmore House (overleaf). It's America's largest private residence, but open to public tours.

The 225-room French Renaissance château was built by George W. Vanderbilt , a young New York aristocrat, on 125,000 secluded acres. Spaniard Rafael Guastavino, one of the designers who assisted chief architect Richard Morris Hunt on the Biltmore project, also worked in town; his 1909 Saint Lawrence's Catholic Church contains the largest unsupported tile dome in the United States.

A baleful beast (above) guards the entrance to the Biltmore Manor. The conservatory (right) is a favorite room for visitors, as is the banquet hall (opposite), where conservators gingerly removed and restored, one at a time, tapestries such as the sixteenth-century Flemish Vulcan and Venus creations. Tapestries were a passion of George Vanderbilt, a world traveler and habitual art collector. Renovation and restoration are ongoing at the gigantic home. Biltmore curators located the French company that created the original, deteriorating, silk and velvet coverings in Edith Vanderbilt's Louis XV–style bedroom (overleaf); they then commissioned exact copies.